Make It Rain Pierogies

The Ultimate Pierogi Cookbook for 2 or More

BY - Zoe Moore

Copyright Notes

Table of Contents

Introduction

We promise you the phrase "pocketful of sunshine" has never made more sense than as you bite into a delicious and well-made pierogi. Pierogis are delicious and come in so many varieties we think it's scientifically impossible to get tired of them. We swear! Why? You can make them out of pretty much anything you want– even leftovers! However, those ones will probably need to wait a little bit because we actually want you to get comfortable with making them before you start experimenting with your own recipes.

When made right, they can be extremely juicy and flavorful, so why wouldn't you want to try making them? You will need to set a bit of time to make them because of all the folding and pleating involved, so we hope you like arts and crafts because it feels a little bit like a DIY project– a very yummy one, though. Since you're already holding this cookbook in your hands, the next thing you have to do is choose a recipe. Which one will we start with?

We've got plum, sausage, mushroom, beef, potato, ham and cheese varieties and more. After you've tried our 30 recipes, then it's time for you to begin experimenting! We promise you won't regret it. The best part? They're freezer friendly, so making a big batch is always helpful if you're looking for something quick to reheat throughout the week. Good luck!

XXXXXXXXXXXXXXXXXXXXXXXXXXXXXXXXXXXXXXXXXX

Recipe 1 - Homemade Pierogi

This is a delicious combination of potatoes and flour, supplying a good source of fiber and carbohydrates.

Yield: 6

Total Prep Time: 1 hour, 5 minutes per batch

List of Ingredients:

- 5 cups all-purpose flour
- 1 tablespoon salt
- 1 cup water
- 3 eggs
- ½ cup softened butter

For the Filling:

- 4 cubed medium potatoes
- 2 chopped onions
- 2 tablespoons butter
- ½ teaspoon salt
- ½ tablespoon pepper

For Serving:

- ¼ cup chopped onion
- 1 tablespoon butter
- Minced parsley

xxxxxxxxxxxxxxxxxxxxxxxxxxxxxxxxxxxxxxxx

How to Cook:

1. Combine the salt and flour in a bowl. Add eggs, water, and butter to the mixture.

2. Blend until the dough ball is set. Add some extra tablespoon if water is needed.

3. Cover the dough and leave it for 15 to 30 minutes.

4. Boil the potatoes in the saucepan on a high flame. Put the potatoes on simmer for 10 to 15 minutes until tender.

5. Sauté onions in the butter in the skillet until they become tender and set aside the onions after that.

6. Now take the boiled potatoes, drain them, and stir them until the steam has vanished. In the large bowl, press them through any mashing tool.

7. In the mixture of salt, pepper, cream cheese, and onion, stir the potatoes.

8. Make 4 parts of the dough and make the surface lightly floured. Now roll one divided part of the dough on the surface and make its thickness up to ⅛ inches.

9. Take a 3 inches circular biscuit cutter floured and cut the rolled dough. Put 2 tablespoons of filling into the circles of dough.

10. Put some water on the filling to seal it after folding it in half.

11. Add batches of the pierogi into boiled water in the Dutch oven over a high flame. Cook the pierogis for 1 to 2 minutes until they are tender and float to the top.

12. Take them out with the slotted spoon, then sauté 4 pierogis in the butter until they become light brown.

13. Make the pierogis of the remaining dough and sprinkle some parsley on it before serving.

Recipe 2 - Potato and Garlic Pierogi

You will love this dish like a fat child loves cake!

Yield: 4

Total Prep Time: 35- 40 minutes

List of Ingredients:

- 1 tablespoon minced fresh chives
- 1/3 cup water
- 12 egg roll wrappers, cut into 4 1/3-inches
- Freshly ground pepper to taste
- ½ cup cream heavy
- 5 tablespoons unsalted butter
- ¼ cup grated sharp cheddar cheese
- Coarse salt to taste
- 6 sliced garlic cloves
- 2½ cups gold potatoes, cut into 1-inch

xxxxxxxxxxxxxxxxxxxxxxxxxxxxxxxxxxxxxxxxxxx

How to Cook:

1. Boil gently garlic, and potatoes in salty water until they get soft. Wash them out, and cross hot garlic and potatoes from a food mill.

2. Mix it in butter, 4 tablespoons, and cheese, put salt and pepper with the season, and mix the cream.

3. Put potato mixture 1 heaping in the cure of each round, lightly put water on the edges, fold them over filling, and seal it properly; carry on this same process with other dough circles.

4. Take out the rest of the butter and water to the nonstick skillet over a medium-low flame; lightly add pierogi to it, and close the skillet for steam, about 5 minutes.

5. Remove cover from skillet and check if pierogi gets golden brown color from both sides.

6. Wait for about 2 minutes per side—peak pierogi with chives.

Recipe 3 - Plum Pierogi

This delicious pierogi is well, and it tastes good. The recipe may bring your sweet memories back.

Yield: 6 to 8

Total Prep Time: 2 hours

List of Ingredients:

- 2 cups thinly sliced sweet plums
- ½ cup sugar
- 3 ½ cups all-purpose flour
- 1 egg
- ½ tablespoon sour cream
- 1 teaspoon salt
- 1/3 cup buttermilk

XXXXXXXXXXXXXXXXXXXXXXXXXXXXXXXXXXXXXXXXXX

How to Cook:

1. In an electric mixer bowl, mix sour cream, buttermilk, egg, water, and salt until they mix very well.

2. Gently add flour to it at a speed maximum of 2 until properly incorporated.

3. Now, put the rest of the flour in it by looking that it is well incorporated.

4. Wait for 15 minutes, then put flour up to 1 tablespoon so your dough may not stick to the bowl.

5. Put aside your dough by covering it with an elastic wrap.

6. Cut the dough into a 3 to 4-inch circle.

7. Put down 2 slices of plum over your dough; now sprinkle sugar on the plums.

8. Seal the edge with the help of your fingers properly.

9. Take a large pan and put 4 quarts of water, bring it to a boil and mix salt in it.

10. Now, cautiously place pierogies in the water, wait for them to float, and cook for more than 1 to 2 minutes. Take them out and drain them well. Sprinkle some sugar in layers of pierogies to keep them from sticking to each other.

11. You may serve it with sour cream.

Recipe 4 - Spinach Pierogi

Cook this charming pierogi for your family and relatives.

Yield: 7

Total Prep Time: 40 minutes

List of Ingredients:

For the Dough:

- 1 egg
- 1 cup water
- ½ teaspoon salt
- 3 cups flour

For the Filling:

- ½ teaspoon salt and pepper
- Nutmeg
- 1 Havarti cheese slice
- ½ cup parmesan cheese
- ¾ cup cream cheese
- 2 cups cooked spinach
- 2 minced garlic cloves
- 1 minced shallot
- 1 tablespoon butter

xxxxxxxxxxxxxxxxxxxxxxxxxxxxxxxxxxxxxxxxxx

How to Cook:

For the Dough:

1. Whisk the salt and flour in a medium-size bowl.

2. Warm the water with butter in a pot until low warm.

3. Add the fluid to the bowl. Whisk the dough with a spoon until combined, roughly

4. Knead the dough until it gets entirely smooth and soft. The dough must be soft and smooth, but if it is hard or rough, add some water and knead it properly again.

5. Cover the dough with plastic foil and leave it for 25 to 30 minutes. Till the dough is on rest, you can prepare to fill.

For the Spinach:

1. Pour garlic and shallot in butter until they get transparent.

2. Mix all left ingredients.

3. Heat till cheeses are correctly melted and mix them well.

4. Gently add pepper, nutmeg, and salt to taste. Now place filling to get cool.

To assemble and cook:

1. Wave around the dough, about 1/8 inch thickness.

2. Do pieces of dough into a large circle, about 3.6 inches.

3. Put spinach mixture on the dough circle, around one tablespoon, fold the circle and seal the edges with the help of a fork.

4. Take a large bowl filled with salted water; bring it to a boil. Gently add pierogi and mix it properly until they float on the surface of the water.

5. With the help of a slotted spoon, remove out pierogi and clear out.

6. To make it tastier, you may sauté pierogi in onions and butter.

Recipe 5 - Sausage Pierogi

This is simple and includes items that are usually used in the kitchen.

Yield: 5

Total Prep Time: 30 minutes

List of Ingredients:

- 1 20-ounce package frozen pierogi
- 1 package turkey sausage, sliced in half inches lengthwise
- 2 tablespoons butter
- 2 tablespoons canola oil
- 1 sliced onion
- 1 package mixed coleslaw
- ½ teaspoon garlic powder
- ¼ teaspoon celery salt
- ¼ teaspoon pepper
- 1 bay leaf

xxxxxxxxxxxxxxxxxxxxxxxxxxxxxxxxxxxxxxxxx

How to Cook:

1. Cook the sausage in a big skillet using 1 teaspoon of oil and butter, respectively.

2. Cook the pierogi according to package instructions. Add other ingredients and cook for 1 to 2 minutes until mixed well.

3. Drain out the pierogi and cook it in another skillet along with butter and oil.

4. Add the sausage mixture and discard the bay leaf.

Recipe 6 - Polish Pierogi

This pierogi is one of the most popular Eastern European foods.

Yield: 4 dozen

Total Prep Time: 1 hour, 15 minutes per batch

List of Ingredients:

For the Dough:

- 4 cups all-purpose flour
- 2 eggs
- ½ cup sour cream
- 1 teaspoon salt
- 2/3 cup warm water

For the Potato Filling:

- ¼ teaspoon salt
- ¼ teaspoon pepper
- 2 tablespoons softened butter
- ¼ cup chopped onions
- ½ pound boiled and mashed potatoes

For the Cheese Filling:

- 1 beaten egg yolk
- ¼ teaspoon salt
- 2 tablespoons melted butter
- 1 cup 4% cottage cheese
- Liquids for cooking
- 3 chicken bouillon cubes
- 8 cups water
- 1 teaspoon canola oil

For the Toppings:

- ½ cup butter
- 1 chopped onion
- 2 cups sliced mushrooms

xxxxxxxxxxxxxxxxxxxxxxxxxxxxxxxxxxxxxxxxxxxx

How to Cook:

1. Mix the flour, eggs, salt, and water in a large bowl to make dough. Knead well and let it set aside for 10 mins.

2. For potato and cheese filling, combine respective ingredients separately and set aside.

3. Make 3 parts of dough. On a floured surface, roll the dough up to 1 inch thickness. Use a 3-inch cutter to make rounds.

4. Now fold the circles from the edges after putting 1 tablespoon of filling in it.

5. Take a large saucepan and mix the bouillon cubes in the water. Also, add some oil.

6. Drop a batch of pierogi in simmering water over medium flame. Remove with a slotted spoon after tender.

7. Add onions in butter melted in a large skillet. Add mushrooms when onions are lightly browned. Cook until tender.

8. Place pierogi on a serving plate and add mushrooms mixture for topping.

Recipe 7 - Pierogi Quesadillas

This delicious dish loaded with tortillas will be a source of joy and nutrition for your loved ones.

Yield: 4

Total Prep Time: 15 minutes

List of Ingredients:

- 24 ounces refrigerated mashed potatoes
- Butter flavored cooking spray
- 8 8-inch flour tortillas
- 1 cup chopped and cooked ham
- ½ cup shredded cheddar cheese

xxxxxxxxxxxxxxxxxxxxxxxxxxxxxxxxxxxxxxxxxx

How to Cook:

1. Heat the mashed potatoes.

2. Moisten one side of tortillas using the cooking spray. Grease the downside of the griddle and put half of the tortillas on it.

3. Spread the mashed potatoes on it. Use ham and cheese for topping. For the remaining tortilla, make the greased side up.

4. Cook until tortillas become golden brown and the cheese is melted. Cook for 2-3 minutes on each side over medium heat.

5. Your delicious pierogi quesadillas are ready to serve.

Recipe 8 - Pierogi Lasagna

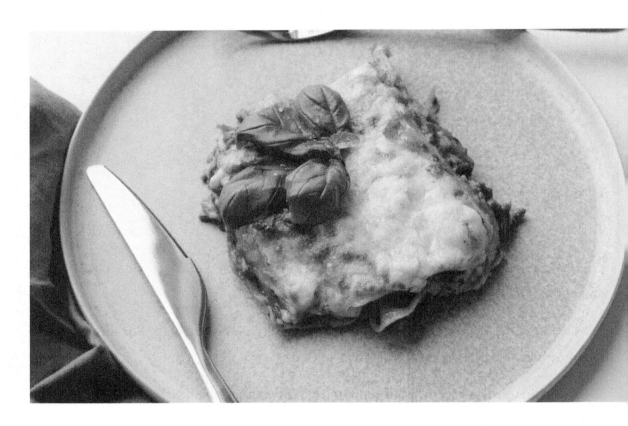

Try this yummy lasagna at your home for your get-together party.

Yield: 12 to 15

Total Prep Time: 1 hour 15 minutes

List of Ingredients:

For the Potato Mixture:

- 8 lasagna noodles
- 6 potatoes
- 2 cups cheddar cheese
- ½ cup margarine
- 1 teaspoon salt
- ½ teaspoon garlic salt

For the Cheese Mixture:

- 1 egg
- ½ teaspoon garlic powder
- 2 1/8 cups ricotta cheese
- ½ cup parmesan cheese

For the Top Layer:

- ¼ cup onion
- ¾ cup cooked chopped bacon
- ¼ oil

xxxxxxxxxxxxxxxxxxxxxxxxxxxxxxxxxxxxxxxxxxx

How to Cook:

1. Prepare the lasagna noodles by following package directions.

2. Now, take a pot full of water, add potatoes, place it on medium-low flame, and bring it to boil after softening them. Drain them out and peel off them.

3. Mash them properly and add marble cheese, salt, and margarine.

4. Stir the ricotta cheese, egg, garlic powder, and parmesan cheese.

5. Turn by turn, put three noodles, then put cheese mixture, three noodles, then potato mixture, then two noodles on the peak.

6. Now, bake it at 370°F for 40 to 45 minutes. Before serving, wait for 10 minutes.

Recipe 9 - Lazy Pierogi

If you are looking for something easy to cook and nutritious, this dish is perfect for you to make.

Yield: 10

Total Prep Time: 15 minutes, 5 minutes for each batch

List of Ingredients:

- 2 eggs
- 1 ¼ cups all-purpose flour
- 1 teaspoon salt
- 1 chopped onion
- 2 cups cottage cheese
- 2 cups cream curd
- 1 cup sour cream
- 3 tablespoons melted butter

xxxxxxxxxxxxxxxxxxxxxxxxxxxxxxxxxxxxxxxxxx

How to Cook:

1. Mix the cottage cheese and eggs in a large bowl. Add flour, salt, and 1 tablespoon of butter.

2. Bring 2 quarts of water to boil in a Dutch oven.

3. Drop pierogi in the simmering water in batches for 4 to 6 minutes.

4. Let pierogi cool down on a towel paper after putting them out using a slotted spoon.

5. Sauté onions and pierogi in the remaining butter using a large skillet. Put pierogi into dishes when they become light brown.

6. Use the sour cream to serve.

Recipe 10 - Cherry Pierogi

This sweet pierogi is filled with sweet juicy cherries, which is mouthwatering!

Yield: 8

Total Prep Time: 50 - 55 minutes

List of Ingredients:

- ½ tablespoon salt
- ½ cup sugar
- 2 cups pitted cherries
- 1 prepared pierogi dough

xxxxxxxxxxxxxxxxxxxxxxxxxxxxxxxxxxxxxxxxxxx

How to Cook:

For the Cherry Vareniki:

Cut out round dough pieces, about 3 cm in diameter, put 1/4 teaspoon sugar in the core of the round dough pieces, and put cherries on the peak of sugar. Fold the dough to make a half-moon shape and pinch its edges with the help of your finger. Seal them tightly.

For the Cherry Pelmeni:

1. Use 1 cherry and 1/4 sugar.

2. You can make diaper shape. Place pierogi on a lightly floured surface until they are ready.

3. Take a pot filled with salty water and bring it to a boil for about 3 minutes. Wait for the pierogi to start floating on the surface of the water wait more than 2 minutes, and take them out.

4. Dust some sugar on pierogies to keep them sticking. Serve it with sour cream.

Recipe 11 - Sauerkraut Pierogi

This pierogi is filled with sauerkraut, onion, and mushrooms, which will taste yummier!

Yield: 24

Total Prep Time: 35 to 37 minutes

List of Ingredients:

- ½ cup butter
- 1 chopped onion
- 1 cup chopped mushrooms
- Sauerkraut
- Freshly ground black pepper and salt

xxxxxxxxxxxxxxxxxxxxxxxxxxxxxxxxxxxxxxxxxxx

How to Cook:

1. Blend sauerkraut in a food processor.

2. Transfer to pan or skillet; stir and cook over medium-low flame until smooth and softened. Cook over 8 to 10 minutes. Drain well in a colander.

3. Put butter on a skillet and heat it properly. Gradually add mushrooms and onion. Stir and cook until onions are translucent, about 8 minutes.

4. Now combine onion mixture with sauerkraut, mix pepper, and salt and cook for 3 minutes; place it on the; plate to get cool completely.

Recipe 12 - Pierogi Casserole

This cheesy casserole is very easy to make and very delicious to eat.

Yield: 12

Total Prep Time: 20 minutes, 25 minutes for baking

List of Ingredients:

- 1 cup chopped onion
- ¼ cup butter
- 2 cups drained 4% cottage cheese
- 1 egg
- 1 teaspoon onion salt
- 2 cups mashed potatoes
- ¼ teaspoons salt
- 1/8 teaspoons pepper
- 9 cooked and drained lasagna noodles

xxxxxxxxxxxxxxxxxxxxxxxxxxxxxxxxxxxxxxxxx

How to Cook:

1. Sauté onions in the butter in a skillet. Set aside.

2. Mix cottage cheese, egg, and onion salt in a bowl.

3. Mix potatoes, 2/3 cups of cheese, salt, and pepper in another bowl.

4. Take a 13×9 inches baking dish and put 3 noodles in it after greasing. Use cottage cheese mixture and 3 more noodles for topping.

5. Use sautéed onions, potato mixture, and remaining noodles to top it. Use ⅓ cup cheese to top.

6. Bake for 25 to 30 mins at 350°F. Serve after standing for 10 minutes.

Recipe 13 - Pierogi with Italian Plum Filling with Pickled Red Cabbage and Spiced Sour Cream

Make this yummy dish for your dinner table!

Yield: 5- 8

Total Prep Time: 1 hour 15minutes

List of Ingredients:

- Basic pierogi

For the Italian Plum Filling:

- 2 tablespoons sugar
- 24 Italian plums

For the Spiced Sour Cream:

- ¼ teaspoon fresh nutmeg
- ½ teaspoon vanilla extract
- 3 tablespoons sugar confectioners
- 1 cup sour cream

xxxxxxxxxxxxxxxxxxxxxxxxxxxxxxxxxxxxxxxx

How to Cook:

1. Cut a split into plum; place out pits. Fill chambers of plum with sugar. Plums should be closed while putting in sough. Utilize one plum for one pierogi.

2. Stir sour cream, nutmeg, sugar, and vanilla extract. Before serving, chill it properly.

Recipe 14 - Pierogi Skillet

This unique and delicious combination will make your mouth water.

Yield: 12

Total Prep Time: 10 minutes, 1 ½ hours for cooking

List of Ingredients:

- ½ lb. bacon
- 1 chopped onion
- 27 ounces rinsed and squeezed dry sauerkraut
- 1 shredded cabbage
- ½ teaspoon pepper
- 5 cups uncooked egg noodles
- 6 tablespoons butter
- 1 ½ teaspoons salt

xxxxxxxxxxxxxxxxxxxxxxxxxxxxxxxxxxxxxxxxxxx

How to Cook:

1. Cook the bacon in a large skillet until it becomes crispy. Add onions to it and cook until onions are tender.

2. Drain and add pepper, sauerkraut, and cabbage. Mix it well and put it on simmer for 45 minutes

3. Cook the noodles and stir the cabbage mixture, salt and butter into it.

4. Put it on simmer for around 30 minutes and serve.

Recipe 15 - Parsnip Pierogi with Pickled Red Cabbage and Sautéed Apples

Make this pierogi whenever you get free time. Freeze it for up to 3 months and enjoy!

Yield: 6 to 8

Total Prep Time: 1 hour

List of Ingredients:

- 2 apples
- 2 teaspoons unsalted butter
- ¼ cup farmer's cheese
- 2 teaspoons prepared horseradish sauce
- Freshly grated nutmeg
- Fresh salt and black pepper
- 1 teaspoon unsalted butter
- 2 shallots
- 2 ½ cups parsnips
- 2 ¼ cups all-purpose flour
- 1 ½ tablespoons sour cream
- 1 egg
- Salt and black pepper
- ¼ shredded red cabbage
- 1 teaspoon crushed caraway seeds
- 1 ½ tablespoons sugar
- ¼ cup red wine vinegar

xxxxxxxxxxxxxxxxxxxxxxxxxxxxxxxxxxxxxxxxxxx

How to Cook:

1. To build red-cabbage slaw, mix sugar, caraway seeds, and vinegar in a bowl. Sling in cabbage.

2. Now add Season with pepper and salt. Soak it for one to two hours or overnight.

3. Whisk the salt and flour in a medium-size bowl.

4. Warm the water with butter in a pot until low warm.

5. Add the fluid to the bowl. Whisk the dough with a spoon until combined, roughly

6. Knead the dough until it gets entirely smooth and soft. The dough must be soft and smooth, but if it is hard or rough, add some water and knead it properly again.

7. Cover the dough with plastic foil and leave it for 25 to 30 minutes. Till the dough is on rest, you can prepare to fill.

8. For the moment ready the filling, take saucepan filled with salted water and place parsnips in it. Boil it and wait until it softens 15-20 minutes.

9. Take them out and place them into a food mill to get a puree.

10. Put butter and shallots in another pan and wait for shallots to get soft, mix from time to time, about two to three minutes.

11. Mix shallots into the puree, and add on salt, pepper, and nutmeg. Pick up from the heat and left it to get cool. Then stir cheese and horseradish.

12. Cut the dough into 2 pieces, form it into a ball. Roll the ball until 1/8 inch. Using the cup or glass, cut the dough into a circle. Do the same with the remaining dough.

13. To fill it, take a dough circle and place it lightly. Put 1 tablespoon of filling, put it in the mid of the dough, and to seal it, pinch its edges, use your finger all around it to seal it completely.

14. I want to make sautéed apples, put a pan over medium-low flame. First, heat butter and gently add apple slices in it, and sling to coat.

15. Mix sugar in it and stir very well. Wait until slices get brown.

16. If it is ready to serve, take a bowl put salted water, and boil it. Lightly add pierogi in it and stir slowly.

17. When the pierogi start floating, wait for 2 minutes and take them out.

18. Serve it with sautéed apples and red- cabbage slaw.

Recipe 16 - Pierogi Chicken Supper

This delicious recipe takes just 30 minutes and gives a healthy addition to your table.

Yield: 4

Total Prep Time: 30 minutes

List of Ingredients:

- 1 package frozen pierogi
- 1 pound boneless chicken breast, cut into 2 ×1/2 strips
- ¼ teaspoon salt
- 1/8 teaspoon pepper
- 2 tablespoons butter
- ½ sliced sweet onion
- ½ cup shredded cheddar cheese

xxxxxxxxxxxxxxxxxxxxxxxxxxxxxxxxxxxxxxxxxx

How to Cook:

1. Toss the chicken with salt and pepper. Cook the pierogi according to package instructions and drain it.

2. Sauté chicken and onion in a large non-stick skillet and cook chicken until its pink color fades away. Put it out of the pan.

3. Sauté pierogi in the same pan until light brown in butter.

4. Stir chicken mixture into it and sprinkle cheese on it.

5. Serve after the cheese is melted.

Recipe 17 - Mushroom Pierogi

Serving this pierogi with sour cream and soft brown onions will make your days!

Yield: 3 to 4

Total Prep Time: 1 hour

List of Ingredients:

- 1 tablespoon minced flat-leaf parsley
- 3 tablespoons heavy cream
- 1 teaspoon fresh thyme
- ¼ teaspoon freshly ground black pepper
- 1 teaspoon salt
- 2 tablespoons lemon juice
- ¼ cup minced shallots
- ½ tablespoon olive oil
- ½ tablespoon butter
- 1 ¼ cups white, cremini, or shiitake mushrooms
- 1 pierogi dough

xxxxxxxxxxxxxxxxxxxxxxxxxxxxxxxxxxxxxxxxxx

How to Cook:

1. Separate stems from shiitake mushrooms cut stems of cremini and white mushrooms.

2. Put mushrooms in the food processor for an about eight-time pulse until mushrooms get finely chopped. Place aside.

3. In a pan of medium size, heat oil and butter over the low flame; put shallots. Cover and cook until get softens about 3 minutes.

4. Gently add pepper, salt, mushrooms, and lemon juice, mix it well. Now increase flame and stir it very well for about 6 to 8 minutes until it gets dry.

5. Put in thyme, parsley, cream, and cook for about 2 minutes; now, place it in a medium bowl.

6. For dumplings, put a heaping teaspoon of a filling on the front of a pierogi dough circle.

7. With the help of water, cover the edges with water, now fold in half to form a moon shape, use your fingers to pinch the edges of the semi-circle pierogi. Cover the pierogi after it is done with filling.

8. For the moment, take a pot filled with salted water, bring it to a boil. Add pierogi in it. Boil it lightly until pierogi float to the surface. Cook it more about two minutes.

9. Take them out and repeat this same process with other filled pierogi. For delicious taste, serve quickly.

Recipe 18 - Pierogi Beef Skillet

This yummy mixture of vegetables and beef will let you enjoy your favorite pierogi.

Yield: 4

Total Prep Time: 25 minutes

List of Ingredients:

- 1 pound beef
- ¼ cup all-purpose flour
- ½ cup chopped onions
- ½ teaspoon pepper
- ½ teaspoon Italian seasoning
- 1/8 teaspoon salt
- 1 package frozen pierogi
- 1 20-ounce can beef broth
- 2 cups frozen mixed vegetables
- ½ cup shredded cheddar cheese

xxxxxxxxxxxxxxxxxxxxxxxxxxxxxxxxxxxxxxxxx

How to Cook:

1. Cook beef and onions in a heavy skillet until their pink color fades away. Drain it and reserve with 3 teaspoons of drippings.

2. Stir in the flour and seasoning and gradually stir in broth. Bring it to a boil and cook for 1 to 2 minutes.

3. Cook along with pierogi and vegetables for about 5 minutes.

4. Serve after sprinkling cheese on it.

Recipe 19 - Pumpkin Pierogi

One cannot sleep well, love well, and think well if he has not dined well. So, if you are in the mood for something special, then cook this dish.

Yield: 20

Total Prep Time: 1 hour 8 minutes

List of Ingredients:

- 1 handful fresh sage
- 6 tablespoons unsalted butter
- ¼ teaspoon freshly grated nutmeg
- Pepper and kosher salt
- 1/3 cup ricotta cheese
- 1/3 cup freshly grated parmesan cheese
- 2/3 cup pumpkin puree
- 1 tablespoon vegetable oil
- 1 egg yolk
- 1 egg
- 1 cup plain Greek yogurt
- 1 tablespoon melted unsalted butter
- 2 ¼ cups all-purpose flour
- 1 teaspoon salt

xxxxxxxxxxxxxxxxxxxxxxxxxxxxxxxxxxxxxxxxxxx

How to Cook:

1. Whisk the salt and flour in a medium-size bowl.

2. Warm the water with butter in a pot until low warm.

3. Add the fluid to the bowl. Whisk the dough with a spoon until combined, roughly

4. Knead the dough until it gets entirely smooth and soft. The dough must be soft and smooth, but if it is hard or rough, add some water and knead it properly again.

5. Cover the dough with plastic foil and leave it for 25 to 30 minutes. Till the dough is on rest, you can prepare to fill.

6. Take the food processor bowl, and mix the parmesan, ricotta cheese, pumpkin, a pinch of nutmeg, salt, and pepper in it.

7. For the moment, divide the dough into two pieces, and roll one piece until it gets very thin about 1/6 inch.

8. Now, with the help of a glass or round cutter, cut out dough in a circle, and do it again with the remaining dough.

9. With the help of a spoon, put a filling in mid of the dough circles. Outline the dough circle with water, seal them and press them from the edges properly.

10. Now, you can easily boil pierogi or freeze them.

11. For freezing, you can put pierogi on a baking sheet for at least 25-55 minutes. After that, you can put pierogies on a sealable bag and freeze them for at least 2 to 3 months.

12. If you want to eat frozen pierogi, you can take them out, put them in a pot full of salted water, and bring them to boil until pierogi start floating on the surface of the water.

13. For making crunchy pierogi, you can heat the skillet over a low-medium flame and put butter in it.

14. Cook and mix it for two to three minutes until pierogi appear brown. Put them in boiled pierogi in about a single layer.

15. Cook for a few minutes more so that pierogi may get crunchier and crispier.

16. Serve it quickly with crispy sage and butter, brown from the skillet.

Recipe 20 - Pierogi Pasta Shells

This is the best combination of pasta and pierogi, which is a favorite among all ages.

Yield: 17

Total Prep Time: 30 minutes, 30 minutes for each batch

List of Ingredients:

- 51 jumbo pasta shells
- 3 packages mashed potatoes
- 2 tablespoons minced and dried onions
- ½ teaspoon onion powder
- ½ teaspoon garlic powder
- 4 cups shredded cheddar cheese
- ½ cup chopped green onions

xxxxxxxxxxxxxxxxxxxxxxxxxxxxxxxxxxxxxxxx

How to Cook:

1. Cook the package of pasta shells and rinse in cold water.

2. Take a microwave-safe bowl and put the mashed potatoes in it. Microwave for 4 minutes and stir once.

3. Add the garlic and onion powder to minced onions and stir 2 cups of cheese and blend well.

4. Take two 13×9 inches baking dishes and put the stuffed mixture of shells.

5. Sprinkle the cheese and chopped green onions on it. Bake for 20 minutes at 350°F.

6. Bake again for 10 minutes until heated through.

7. Serve the delicious pasta shell mixture.

Recipe 21 - Pierogi Supper

This is a very filling and healthy dish that takes only 15 minutes to cook.

Yield: 4 to 5

Total Prep Time: 15 to 18 minutes

List of Ingredients:

- 3 tablespoons butter
- 1 zucchini, cut into slices
- ½ teaspoon garlic powder
- 1 yellow squash, cut into slices
- 2 cups cooked ham cubes
- 1 package frozen pierogi

xxxxxxxxxxxxxxxxxxxxxxxxxxxxxxxxxxxxxxxxx

How to Cook:

1. You can cook pierogi by following the directions on the package.

2. Take a large skillet, and cook the squash, garlic powder, ham, and zucchini in butter for 5 minutes.

3. Take out pierogi and put it in a skillet; heat it lightly.

Recipe 22 - Pork Chops 'n' Pierogi

Surprise your folks by serving this mouthwatering dish on any family occasion.

Yield: 2 to 3

Total Prep Time: 30 minutes

List of Ingredients:

- ¼ cup vinegar cider
- ¼ cup sugar
- 1 sliced golden apple
- 1 sliced onion
- 4 tablespoons butter
- ½ teaspoon pepper
- ½ teaspoon salt
- 1 cup beef chops, ¾ -inch thick
- 8 frozen onion and potato pierogies

xxxxxxxxxxxxxxxxxxxxxxxxxxxxxxxxxxxxxxxxx

How to Cook:

1. Prepare pierogi according to package instructions. For the moment, dust beef chops with ¼ teaspoon pepper and 1/4 teaspoon salt. In a skillet, put 2 tablespoons of butter and heat it. Now add beef chops to it and cook on medium-low flame until water is removed and gets warm.

2. In that skillet, gently add apple slices and fry them until getting soft. Mix in the salt, pepper, sugar, and vinegar—less the heat. Remove the cover after five minutes. Take out pierogi. Put pierogi and beef chops in skillet: mix them to coat.

Recipe 23 - Ham and Cheddar Pierogi Bake

Bake this charming dish and take it to your family gathering dinner table. Everyone will love it!

Yield: 6 to 8

Total Prep Time: 1 hour 10 minutes

List of Ingredients:

- 2 tablespoons thinly sliced green onions
- 1 cup cubed ham
- 1 tablespoon water
- 1 package frozen cheddar and potato cheese pierogies
- 1 ½ cups shredded cheddar cheese
- ¾ cup milk
- ¾ cup chicken broth
- 2 tablespoons all-purpose flour
- 1 cup diced onions
- 2 tablespoons butter

XXXXXXXXXXXXXXXXXXXXXXXXXXXXXXXXXXXXXXXXX

How to Cook:

1. Spray glass dish with cooking spray. Heat an oven to 340 to 350°F.

2. Melt butter in a saucepan, put onions in it, and cook for 4 to 5 minutes; mix it when they get softens.

3. Gently add flour and stir it very well; cook for 4 to 5 minutes when the mixture is bubbly.

4. In cups, mix milk and broth. Quickly mix the mixture of broth in the pan. You may increase flame to medium-high flame and mix very well. Boil them and mix for more than 2 minutes; bring down the flame.

5. Add cheddar cheese 1 cup in it. Stir until fully melted. After that, remove from heat.

6. For the moment, take out frozen pierogies and cover those with elastic wrap in a dish. Microwave them for high 2 minutes. After that, pour cheese sauce on pierogies.

7. Top them with ham and remaining cheese.

8. Bake those 15 to 20 minutes and check that the edges are bubbly. Now, wait for more than 10 minutes. You may top it with green onions.

Recipe 24 - Sweet Cheese Pierogi

This is a recipe with such a charming taste!

Yield: 4

Total Prep Time: 1 hour 45 minutes

List of Ingredients:

For the Dough:

- ½ cup + 1 tablespoon water
- 1.5 tablespoons butter
- 2 cups flour
- ½ teaspoon salt

For the Filling:

- 2 egg yolks
- ¼ cup sugar
- 2 ¼ cups farmer's cheese
- 1 tablespoon vanilla pudding powder
- 1 teaspoon vanilla extract

XXXXXXXXXXXXXXXXXXXXXXXXXXXXXXXXXXXXXXXXXX

How to Cook:

1. Whisk the salt and flour in a medium-size bowl.

2. Warm the water with butter in a pot until low warm.

3. Add the fluid to the bowl. Whisk the dough with a spoon until combined, roughly

4. Knead the dough until it gets fully smooth and soft. The dough must be soft and smooth, but if it is hard or rough, add some water and knead it properly again.

5. Cover the dough with plastic foil and leave it for 25 to 30 minutes. Till the dough is on rest, you can prepare to fill.

6. Stir sugar and egg yolks until it combined properly.

7. Add all the other ingredients and mix them with a mixer or fork.

8. Divide the dough into 2 parts, and cut out rounds with a pierogi cutter.

9. Scoop some filling on each round, and fold the over filling to create a half-circle shape. Press the edges with fingers.

10. Place it under a kitchen towel after sprinkling some flour on it.

11. Now, take a large pot of salted water to boil.

12. Cook pierogi. When floating on the water surface, cook them for at least 1-3 minutes, then remove them from the water. The cooking time depends on the thickness of the dough.

13. Drain it properly and put them on a plate, and enjoy it!

Recipe 25 - Beet Pierogi

Try this yummy and appetizing dish at your home which will make your family happy!

Yield: 4 to 6

Total Prep Time: 1 hour 30 minutes

List of Ingredients:

- 2 cups all-purpose flour
- ½ cup water
- 1 egg
- ¼ cup finely chopped red onion
- 2 teaspoons margarine
- 1 ½ cups peeled and chopped beets

xxxxxxxxxxxxxxxxxxxxxxxxxxxxxxxxxxxxxxxxxx

How to Cook:

1. Put onion and beets in a pan and place them over a medium-high flame; pour 1 cup water in the pan and after one boil, reduce the flame. And wait until beets get tender, for about 10-15 minutes. Take out the water from vegetables and put it in the food processor bowl. Start the machine and add margarine wait till beets get finely chopped.

2. Mix water and egg until mixed properly. After that, mix in flour. Now take out the dough on the little floured surface, and knead it until elastic and smooth, 6 to 9 minutes.

3. Cut the dough into 2 pieces, and form it into a ball. Roll the ball until 1/8 inch. Using the cup or glass, cut the dough into a circle. Do the same with the remaining dough.

4. To fill it, take a dough circle and place it lightly. Put 1 tablespoon of beet filling, put it in the mid of the dough, and to seal it, pinch its edges, and use your finger all around it to seal it completely. Sprinkle some flour on pierogi.

5. Now, take water and fill the pot and boil it. Lightly put pierogies into the water and mix them very lightly to avoid sticking. Wait until pierogies float on the top of the water, around 6 minutes. Take them out and serve with some sour cream on them.

Recipe 26 - Potato and Pea Pierogi

Enjoy this brighter and lighter flavor recipe with your friends.

Yield: 4

Total Prep Time: 2 hours 20 minutes

List of Ingredients:

- 1 tablespoon sour cream
- 1 whisked lightly egg
- Yellow cornmeal for dusting
- 1 cup fresh peas
- 1 ½ unsalted butter sticks
- ¼ cup cream cheese
- Freshly ground pepper and coarse salt
- 2 potatoes
- 2 ½ cups all-purpose flour
- ½ cup milk

xxxxxxxxxxxxxxxxxxxxxxxxxxxxxxxxxxxxxxxxxx

How to Cook:

1. In a bowl, mix sour cream and egg. Mix in 1/2 cup water and milk. Gently whisk in flour until a light dough forms.

2. Now place the dough on the lightly floured surface, and fold the dough to knead until the dough is no stickier.

3. Take a pot and put potatoes with salted water in it. Bring it to a boil over high-medium; cook for 20 to 25 minutes. Drain it and mix properly cream cheese and melted butter. Add 1/4 tablespoons pepper and 1¼ teaspoons salt.

4. Now, prepare an ice bath. Bring a pot of water, salted to boil over a high-medium flame, gradually add peas, cook for at least 4 to 7 minutes, and transfer it to an ice bath. Drain it and put it in a potato mixture.

5. Divide dough into two pieces, and cut out 3-inch circles.

6. Place 1 tablespoon filling in the mid of each circle. Hold one circle in your hand, and fold the dough over, filling to form a crescent. Use fingers to seal the edges.

7. Melt butter sticks into a pan over low-medium flame until dark golden brown for 7 to 10 minutes.

8. Now transfer pierogi to boiling water. Once they float on the water, cook until 2 minutes. Overlay a platter with half brown butter and transfer pierogi to the platter. Sprinkle some salt and brown butter.

Recipe 27 - Smothered Pierogi

This versatile recipe will make your day!

Yield: 4

Total Prep Time: 45 minutes

List of Ingredients:

- ¼ cup grated Romano cheese
- 1 cup shredded mozzarella cheese
- 2.5 cups frozen pierogies
- Salt and black pepper to taste
- 1 pinch crushed red pepper
- 1/8 teaspoon dried oregano
- 1/8 teaspoon dried basil
- ½ teaspoon garlic powder
- 3 teaspoons dried parsley
- 1 can drained mushrooms
- 2 minced garlic cloves
- 1 sliced red bell pepper
- 1 sliced green bell pepper
- 1 sliced onion
- 1 tablespoon olive oil
- 1 cup sausage

xxxxxxxxxxxxxxxxxxxxxxxxxxxxxxxxxxxxxxxxxxx

How to Cook:

1. Heat a skillet over a high- medium flame and mix in the sausage. Mix and cook until color changes from pink to brown, crumbly. After this, remove the sausage from the skillet and put it in the bowl.

2. Heat a skillet and put 1 tablespoon olive oil in it. Mix the red pepper, green pepper, and onion; cook and wait for peppers to get tender and onions to get golden brown color, about 6 minutes. Now stir in mushrooms and garlic; cook for 2 minutes.

3. Now add season with parsley, oregano, red pepper flakes, basil, and garlic powder. Season to taste pepper and salt, and mix them properly. Put vegetables in the sausage bowl and mix them.

4. Heat the large skillet over a medium-high flame and put 1 tablespoon olive oil in it. Heat it. Now take pierogies and put in hot oil, cook till color changes to a golden brown, about 6 minutes.

5. Place sausage and vegetables on the pierogies with the help of a spoon. Dust over it with Romano cheese and mozzarella cheese, and cook and cover until the cheese is fully melted.

Recipe 28 - Vegan Pierogi with Spicy Red Lentil and Sun-Dried Tomato Filling

Cook this delicious vegan pierogi with red lentil and sun-dried tomato filling for your family and win their love.

Yield: 5

Total Prep Time: 1 hour 30 minutes

List of Ingredients:

- 1 pierogi dough without egg
- 4 teaspoons vegetable oil
- ½ cup water
- 1 tablespoon salt
- 2 cups flour

For the Filling:

- 1 teaspoon pepper
- 2 to 3 tablespoons oil
- 12 sun-dried tomatoes
- 2 garlic cloves
- 1 onion
- ¼ teaspoon cayenne pepper
- ½ teaspoon turmeric
- ¼ teaspoon cumin
- 1 teaspoon dried thyme
- 1 teaspoon paprika powder
- 1 cup red lentil
- 1 cup vegetable broth

xxxxxxxxxxxxxxxxxxxxxxxxxxxxxxxxxxxxxxxxxxxx

How to Cook:

For the Pierogi dough:

1. Whisk the salt and flour in a medium-size bowl.

2. Warm the water with butter in a pot until low warm.

3. Add the fluid to the bowl. Whisk the dough using the spoon until combined, roughly

4. Knead the dough until it gets entirely smooth and soft. The dough must be smooth and soft, but if it is hard or rough, add some water and knead it properly again.

5. Cover the dough with plastic foil and leave it for 25 to 30 minutes. Till the dough is on rest, you can prepare to fill.

For the Filling:

6. Cook the lentils; wash in the sieve and add to the pot, put into broth, then cover.

7. Bring it to boiling on medium; low flame and cook it for a minimum of 10 minutes until they are soft. Wash them and mash them with the fork.

8. Cut the onion into small pieces, and chop your tomatoes sun-dried and garlic finely.

9. Heat oil in the pan, add spices (turmeric, cumin, thyme, cayenne pepper, paprika powder), cook them till 8 minutes after putting garlic in them, then cook for more than 1 to 2 minutes.

10. Now mix the lentils cooked with onion and dried tomatoes. Add pepper and season using salt. Add oil 2 to 3 tablespoons from the jar of tomatoes so that the filling does not dry.

11. Now put a scoop of the filling in these pierogi and seal edged properly with fingers.

12. Cook those pierogi in salty water with more amount. After some time, they will float on the water and cook for more than 2 minutes. Take it out from the slotted spoon.

13. They taste good pan-fried in butter/ oil/ ghee.

14. Enjoy it!

Recipe 29 - 18 Pierogi Pizza

Bake this delicious pizza at your home and enjoy the charming taste with your family and folks.

Yield: 10- 12

Total Prep Time: 2 hours 20 minutes

List of Ingredients:

For the Pizza Dough:

- ¼ cup olive oil
- 1 teaspoon salt
- 3 cups all-purpose flour
- 1 cup warm water
- 2 teaspoons sugar
- 2 ¼ teaspoons active dry yeast

For the Toppings:

- ¼ cup bacon bits
- 6 thinly sliced potatoes
- 2 tablespoons olive oil
- 1 bunch chopped green onion
- 1 cup cheese
- 2 tablespoons garlic powder
- 1 cup sour cream

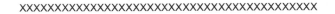

xxxxxxxxxxxxxxxxxxxxxxxxxxxxxxxxxxxxxxxxxxxxx

How to Cook:

1. Take a small bowl, and dissolve sugar and yeast in warm water. Wait for 5 minutes for the yeast to begin and form bubbles.

2. Mix salt and flour in a bowl; put ¼ cup olive oil and yeast mixture over the flour. Combine and knead until dough forms for about 4 to 7 minutes. Now transfer the dough to a little oiled bowl and cover it with a kitchen towel and place it in a warm place; wait for the dough to rise or double in size for about 50 minutes to 1 hour.

3. Take a pot, put tomatoes in it, and cover tomatoes with water. Bring water to a boil, cook for 10 minutes until tomatoes get soft, and clear out tomatoes from the water.

4. Take a large skillet, pour 2 tablespoons oil olive over a high-medium flame; gently add potatoes until they change their color to light golden, and cook for about 5 to 8 minutes.

5. Now, preheat the oven to 390°F.

6. Take a small bowl, and mix garlic powder and sour cream to ready pizza 'sauce.'

7. Quickly stretch pizza dough on the pizza stone for about a 12-inch circle. Now expand the sauce all over the pizza dough. Sprinkle tomatoes to cover the dough. Dust, green onion, bacon bits, and cheddar cheese on top.

8. Bake pizza in the oven, preheated until the crust of pizza gets golden brown, 15 to 19 minutes.

Recipe 30 - Blueberry Pierogi

Try this sweet pierogi at your home and serve it as an after-dinner dessert. To make it more delicious, you may sprinkle melted butter, sour cream, and some blueberries on top.

Yield: 80

Total Prep Time: 1 hour 10 minutes

List of Ingredients:

For the Filling:

- 5 cups blueberries
- ½ cup white sugar

For the Dough:

- 8 cups all-purpose flour
- 2 eggs
- 6 tablespoons unsalted butter
- 2 cups water or as needed

xxxxxxxxxxxxxxxxxxxxxxxxxxxxxxxxxxxxxxxxxx

How to Cook:

For the Pierogi Dough:

1. Whisk the salt and flour in a medium-size bowl.

2. Warm the water with butter in a pot until low warm.

3. Add the fluid to the bowl. Whisk the dough with a spoon until combined, roughly

4. Knead the dough until it gets entirely smooth and soft. The dough must be soft and smooth, but if it is hard or rough, add some water and knead it properly again.

5. Cover the dough with plastic foil and leave it for 25 to 30 minutes. Till the dough is on rest, you can prepare to fill.

For the Filling:

6. Fill up the dough circle with 1 tablespoon of blueberries and dust of sugar. Fold the dough over into a half-circle shape and use your fingers to seal it properly edges.

7. Now, take a large pan full of salted water, and boil pierogi until 5 to 8 minutes. After they start floating in the water, cook for 2 minutes. Drain them with the help of a colander.

About the Author

From a young age, Zoe loved being in the kitchen! More specifically, her uncle's bakery. Despite not actually working there, she would sit on the working table and watch herself get covered in flour over the next couple of hours. She also watched closely as her uncle kneaded the dough, measured out ingredients, and even decorated cakes. Even though she never tried doing it herself, she could recite the steps to most of the baked goods sold like her favorite song.

It wasn't until her 16th birthday, though, that she realized just how much she wanted to dedicate her life to making desserts too. No matter how much Zoe's mom insisted on buying a beautiful cake from a local bakery for her Sweet 16 party, Zoe wouldn't budge. She wanted to make the cake herself, and she did. Even though it wasn't the prettiest of cakes, it tasted delicious! Her whole family still remembers the flavor combo to this day: pistachio and orange cake. From there, things only got better!

After graduating from culinary school, Zoe worked in some of the finest bakeries throughout Europe. She wanted to learn from the best. Eventually, however, she decided to go back home and start her own business in Chicago, near her friends and family. That business is now one of the nicest bakeries in the city, which she has run with the help of her best friend, Lola, since 2015

Author's Afterthoughts

Hi there!

This is me trying to thank you for supporting my writing by purchasing my cookbook. I can't begin to express how much it means to me! Even though I've been doing this for quite a while now, I still love to know that people enjoy making my recipes, and I like to thank them for it personally.

You see, without you, my job would be meaningless. A cook with no one to eat their food? A cookbook author with no one to read their book? I need you to love my work to be rewarding, so do you?

One of the biggest ways to thank you for supporting me is by asking what you like or dislike most about my books. Are the recipes easy to follow? Do you think I should write more baking books, or what would you like to see more of? I will get to your suggestions for new books and improvements soon, ready to use them for my next book — so don't be shy!

THANK YOU.

ZOE MOORE

Made in the USA
Coppell, TX
07 June 2023

17792460R00050